a 7 week study
brought to you by p31 fitness

ISBN-13: 978-0692137413 (P31 Fitness)
ISBN-10: 0692137416

Book Layout by Evangela.com
Book design by Brenda Cicchini

Printed in the United States of America.

First printing edition 2018.

P31 Fitness
3960 FM 981
Leonard,TX 75452

www.p31fitness.com/worthit

TABLE OF CONTENTS

introduction

In today's world teenage girls can have a reputation for being clique-ish and catty, petty and mean. Our world is telling them to think a certain way, act a certain way, dress a certain way, and if they don't, then they are just not enough. We want to thank you for your willingness to love and mentor this next generation of teen girls. P31 Fitness as a whole is based around community; a safe place for women to come and be real. But depending on how well your girls know one another, you may still have some work to do to establish a community of trust and openness. We hope to have modeled in this book and video series women sharing their struggles to encourage one another, and we pray that your group can do the same with the tools we have provided. Our hope is that through your willingness to step out in faith to lead this group, that teens will learn their worth in Christ and grow to know the Lord on a personal level.

We encourage you to enlist help, teaching this group with a partner, so that you can model spiritual friendship and openness with sins and struggles. This will also give you a prayer partner on this journey. As a reminder, you may have girls in your group who do not know much about God or the Bible. That is okay; in fact, it is wonderful! Encourage them that there is nothing wrong with that; we all start somewhere. Create an environment where they can ask questions without being judged. For this reason, we listed Scriptures in the discussion questions in order of the Bible, so it is easier for them to find, and for you to help them find the verses.

Even though this is a seven-session study, we recommend taking eight or nine weeks. This will allow you to have an introduction session where girls can get together to get to know one another and receive their workbooks. Nine weeks will allow you a meeting to conclude the series and potentially do a service project, a suggested activity from Session 7.

The videos can be substituted for each chapter's reading, so that everyone views the lessons together. If you have both the videos and the *Worth It!* books, the videos allow those who did not get to their reading that week to feel like they are still part of the group and not behind. We encourage you to purchase both, as sometimes it takes multiple times to hear something for it to stick. If you have chosen not to purchase the videos, your group

should read Session 1 before they come to their first meeting. They do not need to answer the discussion questions after their reading, because you will discuss those as a group during the meeting time.

After you watch the videos, or highlight the reading, begin discussing the provided questions with the girls. They will explore what the Bible has to say about the particular topic. These questions should cause some valuable self-evaluation. Encourage the girls to be honest and open with one another, creating a safe environment where girls can "bear one another's burdens, and so fulfill the law of Christ" (Galatians 6:2). One of our goals of this project is to foster spiritual friendships among the participants, and mentoring relationships between participants and facilitators.

The Digging Deeper section is for the girls to complete on their own at home during the week. Please do not feel like you need to assign it as homework, but just let the participants know that section is there for those who are ready and willing to dig a little deeper!

You can utilize the coloring graphics and the journaling pages as you see fit during your lesson. Possibly at the end for a time of reflection, or something you encourage the girls to do at home as they ponder all that they have learned.

Be sure to conclude your lesson with the Key Verse, Beauty Tip and Action Challenge. Encourage the girls to complete the Action Challenge throughout the week. These provide for a great check-in for group text messages or other conversations with the girls, or for starting off the discussion the next week. You can also challenge the girls to commit the key verse to memory.

Possible schedule for a 75-90 minute session:

- Welcome girls with background music playing, have them put on name tags (10 min)
- Icebreaker or suggested activity (10-20 min)
- Introduce the lesson for the day, play the video (or summarize the reading) (15-20 min)
- Work through the discussion questions (20 min)
- Go over Key Verse, Beauty Tip, and Action Challenge (5 min)
- Time of quiet reflection to journal or color the graphic in their workbooks (10 min)
- Remind them they can do the Digging Deeper section on their own (1 min)
- Close in prayer (4 min)

Possible schedule for a 45-minute - 1 hour session

- Welcome girls with background music playing, have them put on name tags (5 min)
- Icebreaker or suggested activity (10-15 min)
- Introduce the lesson for the day, play the video (or summarize the reading) (15 min)
- Work through the discussion questions (15 min)

- Go over Key Verse, Beauty Tip, and Action Challenge (5 min)
- Remind them they can do the Digging Deeper section on their own (1 min)
- Close in prayer (5 min)

session one →

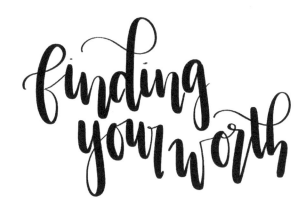

finding your worth

God did not make a mistake when he made you.
You don't need to be anything more.

INTRODUCTION TO TOPIC:

I am not _____ enough. There is something that all of us can insert into that blank. The world today tells us that we do not measure up. We see the beautiful, skinny model on the magazine cover or we see someone's amazing experience on social media, and we immediately compare ourselves to the "perfection" the world portrays. This is not at all how God wants us to view ourselves. The Bible contradicts this over and over. For this lesson, you will study how God views us and wants us to view ourselves. You will spend time teaching the girls that their worth is found in Christ alone.

STRUGGLES AT THIS AGE:

Knowing your worth in Christ can be a struggle at any age, but definitely in the teen years. There are so many things pulling young girls down these days. There are the struggles that have always been there, with popularity, dissatisfaction with personal appearance, and desire for a boyfriend. Internal struggles often clash with external expectations, which come from almost every relationship: parents, teachers, coaches, friends, boyfriends, etc. When teens can't live up to these (often different) expectations, their self-worth deteriorates. Today there is also a whole other level of social media. The "perfection" that is just a click away can be another stressor in young girls' lives.

In a group setting like this, the biggest challenge at this age is enabling the girls to open up. You want to create a safe space for the girls, one where they can feel comfortable enough to share their hearts and know they won't be judged or put down for thoughts they have had or choices they have made. Girls can be so mean, but this group should be a respite from that.

ACTIVITY IDEAS
Before beginning the lesson:

Secret Doubts and Fears
- **Materials Needed:**
    - Two strips of paper for each girl
    - One envelope per girl
- Give girls two strips of paper and an envelope. Have them write on one strip a negative thought they have about themselves and then a negative thought they think others have about them.
- Have the girls put those strips of paper with the negative thoughts in their envelopes, write their names on them, and seal them. Hang on to the envelopes from all the girls until we wrap up the study. * See Session 8

Icebreakers: This first session will be about creating a safe space where everyone is comfortable sharing with one another. Choose one or two of these icebreaker activities to help facilitate that group connection and openness.

Name Game
- **Materials Needed:** none
- Have the girls say their name and an "ing" verb about themselves that starts with the same letter of their name. (Example: Jumping Julie) You can even get real fun and have them act it out. If your group of girls know each other pretty well, they can pick names for each other. Make sure they are positive and encouraging names.

Toilet Paper Fun Facts
- **Materials Needed**
  - Roll of toilet paper
- Pass the roll of toilet paper around and tell girls to tear off some paper for themselves. Don't tell them what it is going to be used for.
- When all girls have some, explain that they will tell the group something about themselves for each square of toilet paper they have.

Two Facts and a Fib
- **Materials Needed:** none
- Have girls think of two facts and a one fib to share about themselves. Then have each girl share the three thoughts. The group must figure out which are the facts and which is the fib.

LEADER DEVOTIONAL:

Key Verse:

For you created my inmost being; you knit me together in my mother's womb. I praise you God, for I am fearfully and wonderfully made. Your works are wonderful, I know that full well.

Psalm 139:13 – 14

As women, this question can often plague our lives: "Am I worth it?" Am I worthy of forgiveness? Am I worthy of friendship? Am I worthy of love? We tend to seek affirmation in one way or another. Let's address how we truly feel about ourselves. Do we feel worthy? Do we treat ourselves as if we are worthy?

Worthy is defined as "having adequate or great merit, character, or value." Could you put your name before that definition and believe those words? Many women struggle in this area. They don't feel like they ever really measure up to some imaginary standard they have created. They continually put themselves down and feel "unworthy." The problem is that how we feel about ourselves, or our self-worth, determines how we treat others, how we act in tough circumstances, and how we live from day to day! We have each been made in God's image. He is worthy of our praise. He made each of us worthy, and it is time to start believing it! You are worthy!

Whatever you "feel" about yourself is just a feeling. The truth is that God made us, loves us, and He calls us. Ladies, let's start believing it! It can make a tremendous difference in our daily lives. Each morning, look in the mirror and say this verse out loud: **"I praise you God, for I am fearfully and wonderfully made."** You may even want to write it on a note card to post on your mirror. The more you say it, the more you believe it, and the more you will feel it. Truth is truth: you are worthy!

In this lesson, you will be challenging the girls in your group to the following a beauty tip and doing an action challenge. We encourage you to do these for yourself first, so you can testify to the girls about what kind of impact they had on you, mentally, emotionally, and spiritually.

action challenge

Everyday when you look in the mirror say something kind about yourself.

beauty tip

When you find yourself thinking *I don't like who I am!* Instead think, *"God created me and loves me in a way that I cannot even begin to fathom."* Let's work on getting to know Him each day and love Him in return.

key takeaways

session two

discovering your purpose

You do not have to be perfect to be used by God.

INTRODUCTION TO TOPIC:
Confidence is a characteristic that can be determined by external approval. The world, our peers, and sometimes even our families can affect the confidence we do or do not have. If we spend time comparing ourselves to others or wishing we were more like someone else, we miss out on the person God has made us to be and the purpose He has for us. God has given us each our own talents, passions, desires, and characteristics—there is no one like us. We need to have confidence in who God has and is making us to be, and walk in His purpose for us.

STRUGGLES AT THIS AGE:
At this age in a girl's life, she is likely not very confident and not sure what her purpose is yet. It is hard to be confident in your purpose when you are still considered young. Teens want independence and to be treated as adults, but struggle, as they are still dependent on parents or guardians in many ways. When they try to become independent, but fail, or have independence taken from them, their confidence falters.

Their search for purpose is often influenced by their peers, and what is acceptable in their social circle.

ACTIVITY IDEAS:

I Got Your Back!
- ◆ **Materials Needed:**
  - ▪ 1 piece of paper per girl (white or construction)
  - ▪ Tape
  - ▪ 1 marker per girl
- ◆ Allow girls to write their name in the very middle of their paper.
- ◆ Tape the paper to each girl's back.
- ◆ Give girls time to walk around and write one specific, godly character trait about each of the girls in your group.
- ◆ When finished, have girls look at all the positive things on their piece of paper. Refer back to this during the lesson today. Again, we want the girls to have confidence in who God has made them to be and is making them to be.

Spiritual Gifts Inventory
- ◆ **Materials Needed:**
  - ▪ Spiritual gifts inventory quiz or self-evaluation. Find one here https://www.youthministrypartners.com/files/uploads/SpiritualGiftsInventory.pdf, or your church may have one for members to use.
- ◆ Discuss with the girls:
  - ▪ What did they find that was a surprise to them?
  - ▪ How do they currently use these gifts in their lives?
  - ▪ Emphasize how the girls can have confidence in their results, that God has gifted each on of them in a special way. Help them see that even if some of the girls got the

same gift, their relationships and personalities make each of them uniquely positioned to use these gifts for God's glory.

◆ Hold on to these or have the girls bring them back for Lesson 7, when you will discuss having a servant heart and using the passions and talents God has given them.

You Are Special

◆ **Materials Needed:**

▪ Children's book "You Are Special" by Max Lucado

◆ Read book aloud to the girls, prefacing it with the fact that it is a children's book, but its message is one that people of all ages need to live out. Ask the girls about the labels people try to stick on them, and how they can refuse to let them define who they are, who God made them to be.

◆ If you like, draw a girl's name to receive the book, encouraging the winner to share this book with someone she would like to mentor.

LEADER DEVOTIONAL:

Key Verse:

But he said to me, 'My grace is sufficient for you, for my power is made perfect in weakness.' Therefore I will boast all the more gladly about my weaknesses, so that Christ's power may rest on me. That is why, for Christ's sake, I delight in weaknesses, in insults, in hardships, in persecutions, in difficulties. For when I am weak, then I am strong.

2 Corinthians 12:9 – 10

The belief that self-confidence is essential for accomplishing your purpose is a misguided one. We need to base our confidence on something stronger than ourselves. Since we can sometimes be tossed about by every wave and wind, it is wise of us to build our lives on the solid rock of God's truth (Matthew 7:24). In this way, we will have God-confidence, basing our lives on His view of us, His love for us, and His blessing in our lives. When we have confidence in Him and His ability, we are able to walk in His purpose for our lives.

Every time we question our lives, our circumstances, or our path in this world, we need to remember that God is in control. If we are obeying Him and are one of His children, then we can rest in the fact that God has a plan for us. It is not a mystery for us to figure out, but a daily, trusting walk beside Christ. He is working on each of us individually, every day. He wants us to know that no matter what we may be facing, He is in the business of perfecting us to His standards until the return of His Son (Philippians 1:6).

Spend some time in prayer. Thank God for who He has made you to be and the passions and talents He has given you. Pray for the girls in your group. Pray for God to help them be confident in the person He has made them to be and the purpose He has for them.

In this lesson, you will be challenging the girls in your group to the following beauty tip and action challenge. We encourage you to do these for yourself first, so you can testify to the girls about what kind of impact they had on your heart, mind, soul, and strength.

action challenge

When you start to compare yourself to others, stop and be thankful for who you are.

beauty tip

Use a dry erase marker to write your favorite verse from this chapter on your mirror. Every time you get ready for the day, read the verse aloud.

key takeaways

session three

becoming strong in the Lord

Looking to God for strength through changes, both outside and inside of me.

INTRODUCTION TO TOPIC:

Change is a way of life. If the girls in your group haven't experienced much change in their lives, they certainly will in years to come. Change comes in many different forms. Some change we can't control, while other changes we may choose to make. Reliance on God during this time is crucial. With so much change during the teen years, girls need to know that God is at work in them. They need to be able to rely on His strength because they may feel weak at this uncertain time in their life. We can be strong, but it comes from dependence on God, not ourselves.

STRUGGLES AT THIS AGE:

Change is not easy. There are many decisions to make during this time in teens' lives. Knowing whose voice to listen to during this time can be hard to decipher. Teens have many voices trying to direct their decisions: parents, friends, teachers, mentors, etc. Many decisions they make during this time in their lives can put them on a path for the future. It can be hard for them to know which route to go, which decision to make. They have a difficult time with doubting themselves and their ability to make choices that affect themselves and others. We want them to have an ongoing relationship with God that gives them strength when times of change inevitably arise.

ACTIVITY IDEAS:

Bearing One Another's Burdens
- **Materials Needed:**
  - Small weights or cans of vegetables or fruits
  - Timer
- Have girls partner up.
- Have one girl in each group hold the weights or cans up in front of their bodies with straight arms, parallel to the ground. Time them for one minute. Tell the girls that they can drop their arms as they feel the need to.
  - Discuss: Was that easy? Hard? What would make it easier?
- Do the activity again with the same person holding the weights or cans. But this time tell the partner to support them by holding their wrists. Time them again for a minute.
  - Discuss: Was it easier this time? Why?
  - Relate this to how we can rely on God and other believers in our journey.

Lift-A-Person*

- Have a volunteer (someone of smaller stature) lie on the ground. Have everyone else gather around her (You'll need at least seven girls to do this, but five may work).
- Have one girl at the volunteer's head and the rest on either side of her body.
- Have them each place four fingers (pointer & middle from each hand) under the volunteer's body.
- On the count of three, lift up the volunteer. Not too high!
    - This is a pretty cool trick! The person's weight is distributed amongst everyone and so each person is only lifting a little bit.
    - This can be an illustration about how God helps us find our strength. The Holy Spirit is our helper and works in ways that seem mysterious.

*This activity has some inherent risk, so please be sensitive to your girls' comfort level and aware of the safety of everyone. Perform it at your own risk.

LEADER DEVOTIONAL:

Key Verse:

Look to the LORD and his strength; seek his face always.

Psalm 105:4

Have you ever found yourself at an all-time low, and only then do you realize how long it has been since you prayed and sought God's strength? We must put the time in day after day to nurture a close relationship with the Lord, as this week's key verse points out. That's how we build our house on the solid rock of Jesus Christ.

"I can do all things through Him who gives me strength" (Philippians 4:13) reminds us of the great power we have available to us if we rely on Jesus. Paul was imprisoned at the time that he wrote the book of

Philippians, and just before verse 13, he says he has "learned to be content in whatever circumstances" he is in (v. 11). Through hunger and need, he learned the secret was to rely wholly on the strength of Jesus through his tough situations.

No matter what you are facing in your life today, remember that God's strength will help us accomplish more than we could ever imagine. We can truly do ALL things through Him!

In this lesson, you will be challenging the girls in your group to the following beauty tip and action challenge. We encourage you to do these for yourself first, so you can testify to the girls about what kind of impact they had on your heart, mind, soul, and strength.

action challenge

Journal a change you have survived,
and how it has made you stronger.

beauty tip

Everyday, tell yourself you are strong
in the Lord and in the power of His
might.

key take aways

session four

keeping yourself pure

understanding I am worth protecting and cherishing.

INTRODUCTION TO TOPIC:

Even as Christ-followers, we can be distracted and easily swayed by outer appearances. We can think people are smarter and funnier just because they're more attractive. We can place our own value in looking good and feeling beautiful. We can fix our hope on men and romance instead of on Christ and heaven. We'd like to make sure that young women hear the truth that their love for God is more beautiful to Him than their outer appearance. His is the only approval we need.

We also want them to consider their choices when engaging with the opposite sex. We need to present ourselves as sanctified. Not only because we want to honor God with our bodies and choices, but also because we want to honor our future husbands with our bodies and choices as well.

STRUGGLES AT THIS AGE:

When it comes to purity and modesty, students are engaged in constant battle to protect their bodies, hearts, and minds. They receive conflicting information from television, social media, and even from inside their own homes. Some parents have no opinion about how their daughters dress or who they date. Some mothers even dress more immodestly than most teenagers! The world tells them that sex is a vehicle toward love and the only way to access sex is to make themselves physically desirable. Popular culture would have them believe that all of their friends are having sex, and that some kinds of sex are more acceptable than others (for example sexting, explicit online conversations, oral sex, and the list goes on!). Because of these ways to engage in sexual acts, some new and some old, the line between pure and impure is more blurry than ever. In addition, many girls have fatherless homes, so they often desire a boyfriend so they can experience the value, safety, and love that every young woman needs.

ACTIVITY IDEAS:

The Ideal Husband
- ◆ **Possible materials needed** (could also just brainstorm and discuss out loud without materials)
  - ▪ Poster board, dry erase board, or chalkboard
  - ▪ Marker, dry erase marker, or chalk
- ◆ As a group, make a list of characteristics that the girls would like to find in a good husband.
- ◆ Emphasize character over looks.

- Ask them why they would value specific things. Answers will vary and may give others some good ideas about things they hadn't previously considered.
- Encourage the girls to make their own individual lists by doing this week's "Digging Deeper."

Modest and Fashionable
- **Materials Needed**
  - Fashion and/or teen magazines
  - Scissors
  - Glue
  - Poster board or heavy paper
- In small groups or as individuals, have them create an outfit that is modest, but still on trend, that they would actually wear. Pretend that money is not a factor, and be sure not to shame anyone who is wearing something you consider immodest.
- Alternatively, have girls divide their paper or poster board into two sections: modest and immodest, and challenge them to find a casual outfit, an athletic outfit, and a dressy outfit that fit in both categories.
- Share their finished posters with the group, letting the group discuss the choices made.
- Ask them if it was an easy or a difficult task to find appropriate and attractive outfits. Chances are, it will be challenging. Let them know that finding cute, trendy outfits in the stores is possible, but it will take more work to find the more modest items.
  - Encourage them to consider spicing up clothing through unique accessories.

LEADER DEVOTIONAL:

Key Verse:
Religion that God our Father accepts as pure and faultless is this ...
to keep oneself unstained by the world.

James 1:27

We make choices everyday that determine what lives in our hearts. If we continually surround ourselves with evil and impurity, we will start to become more evil and impure in our hearts and minds. If we are always hearing bad language, watching crude TV shows, and seeing sexual acts outside marriage, then we tend to become numb to right and wrong. We shouldn't hide in a cave and think that we can protect ourselves from all the bad in the world. However, it is important that when we have a choice to hear or see crude or impure things, that we try to choose "whatever is true, whatever is admirable, whatever is right, whatever is pure, whatever is lovely, whatever is commendable, if there is any excellence, anything worthy of praise, think about these things (Philippians 4:8). If there is an area of your life that is not pure, get yourself away from that situation. Ask God to "create in me a clean heart...and renew a right spirit within me" (Psalm 51:10).

Are we pure in our thoughts, words, actions, and in our lives? We have a choice in our surroundings, our input of information, and our focus each day. Hopefully we see the importance of keeping ourselves "stain-free" from worldly things. Yes, we have to live, work, or deal with ungodly people and situations, but we don't have to walk with them and talk like them.

We don't have to let the world change us. Instead, we can change it. But we must try our best to stay "stain-free!"

In this lesson, you will be challenging the girls in your group to the following beauty tip and action challenge. We encourage you to do these for yourself first, so you can testify to the girls about what kind of impact they had on your heart, mind, soul, and strength.

action challenge

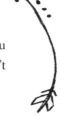

Get rid of TV shows and movies you watch and books you read that don't meet the Philippians 4:8 standard.

beauty tip

Clothe your body to show off your personality, not your body.

key takeaways

session five

being loved

Receiving the great and personal love
God offers each of us.

INTRODUCTION TO TOPIC:

We all seek love, acceptance and security. More often than not, we look for these in the wrong places. We might look for it in sports, academics, friends, personality, physical appearance, boys, etc. We see fictional stories where love overcomes impossible circumstances and obstacles to win the day. We enjoy these stories because of their happy endings. We like to see someone get the love, approval, and acceptance that we ourselves would like to receive. The problem with all of these things is that they are not stable. If we are chasing things that are always changing and moving, then we will never find stability. God is the only thing that won't change.

We hope the girls know, without a doubt after reading this chapter and participating in the group discussion of it, that they are loved by God!

STRUGGLES AT THIS AGE:

The brokenness in the world today makes being loved by God such a difficult concept. The teen years can be an especially hard time to understand this. Families may be broken. Many teens are chasing the approval of others—parents, coaches, teachers, peers, etc.—in order to feel loved. Some may even have been abused, distorting their view of love. They may even feel alone, lost, broken, and rejected. Please read Appendix C on abuse, and Appendix D on bullying, to prepare yourself for leading this week's session. The failure of adults to show godly love, and to lead children to the love of the Lord has devastating results.

The problem is that many do not know what love looks like because they do not receive it from anyone in their lives. So this gives you the opportunity to share with them about God's love for them.

ACTIVITY IDEAS:

I am loved.
- ♦ **Materials Needed:**
  - ▪ Speaker/Music Player
  - ▪ Mirror
  - ▪ Dry Erase board and Marker (or paper and pen)
  - ▪ Extra adult
- ♦ Open your time together with having each student walk to every other student and tell them that they are loved.
  - ▪ *The students may feel uncomfortable at first. Encourage them to take the time with each person to make eye contact, maybe touch their arm, and say, "You are loved." They should really make an effort to mean what they are saying.*

- Play some music, and allow the students to journal or color while individuals participate in the next task.
- Next, you will send the girls, individually, while the others are journaling, into a separate room or private area with an adult, mirror, small white board and a marker.
  - The adult should instruct the student to write the words, "I am loved." on the whiteboard three times.
  - Then they should look at themselves in the mirror and say, "I am loved." three times.
  - *Some girls may just rush through it to because they are uncomfortable. Some will feel silly. Some may struggle to say it because they don't believe it. Encourage them that even though it feels strange, they should try to take it seriously.*
- Once everyone has had a turn in the mirror room, gather them together and ask these questions:
  - Was it easier to tell someone else that they are loved or easier to tell yourself?
    - Why?
  - Was it easier to write it down or say it in the mirror?
    - Why?
  - Why is it so difficult to tell ourselves that we are loved? What keeps us from believing it?

Letter to Self
- **Materials Needed**
  - Girls will need their journals, but have paper and pens or pencils on hand in case anyone doesn't have theirs.
- Have the girls write a letter to themselves. Let them know that no one else will see this letter. Leave it open for them to write anything they would like to write about what they have learned about God or themselves in this chapter. They can also use it as a time to make promises to themselves or to God and to set

goals (spiritual, mental, emotional, and physical). Encourage them to be as detailed as they can and read this letter at least once a week!

LEADER DEVOTIONAL:

Key Verse:

"For God so loved the world, that he gave his only Son, that whoever believes in him should not perish but have eternal life.

John 3:16 ESV

Growing up, when I would read John 3:16, I was always touched by what God has done for us. However, it wasn't until having my own child that I truly understood the power of the words written in the most famous verse in the Bible. Giving up someone so dear and precious to our hearts is something that is difficult to understand for us as humans. God felt the pain of sending His son away from Him. He knew that Jesus would return to heaven one day, but He still felt the separation when Christ came to earth. This should make us realize that the love God has shown to us, by willingly giving His son to die for our sins, is incredibly powerful. May it make us want to do anything and everything that he has asked of us because of His ultimate love.

Think about the impact that God's love has had on your life. Where would you be without His redeeming grace? Without the assurance of His love and acceptance? Consider what it does to your everyday life to live as though you've already been forgiven. Isn't that incredibly powerful? We need to change our perspective as we walk into the world and live as though we are loved.

In this lesson, you will be challenging the girls in your group to the following beauty tip and action challenge. We encourage you to do these for yourself first, so you can testify to the girls about what kind of impact they had on your heart, mind, soul, and strength.

action
challenge

Pray for a safe person with whom you can share your story of brokenness, and then do it.

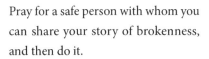

beauty
tip

God loves you in a way that no one else can. Accept His love and rest in it.

key
take aways

session six

receiving peace through prayer

Releasing all my questions and worries to Him.

INTRODUCTION TO TOPIC:

Prayer is a topic that many teens don't understand. We have this amazing access to God through our thoughts and words. He has given us an open door into heaven, where we can bring our hearts to Him. Prayer is a discipline that takes practice and consistency. It is cyclical: the more we pray, the more aligned with His desires we become, and because of that, we pray more.

STRUGGLES AT THIS AGE:

Prayer can be intimidating for teens. They are concerned about doing it wrong or feeling silly. They may feel that their problems, worries, fears, and desires are too insignificant for God to deal with, or too important to release to Him. They may feel that God isn't listening or that He doesn't think they're important enough for Him. We want them to know that even if it doesn't *feel* like He's listening, He really is! He just doesn't always answer in the ways in which we expect.

ACTIVITY IDEAS:

Schedule Prayer
- **Materials Needed:**
  - Girls should use their journals, but have paper and writing utensils on hand in case girls don't have one or forgot it.
- Have girls write out their daily schedules and find a time they can commit to spending with God.
- Encourage the girls wherever they are. If they don't currently spend any time in the Word or in prayer, they need start small, with perhaps five minutes a day or one time a week. If they do already spend some time each week with God, help them commit to more frequent time.

Practice Being Quiet
- **Materials Needed:**
  - Speaker/Music Player
- Play a reverent song and have the girls take their book and Bible to an isolated place. It can be outside (if you have a portable speaker) or somewhere in the room. Give them ten minutes to just be quiet and alone with God. Encourage them to write down any thoughts or prayers that may come to mind, or just close their eyes and shut off their mind to experience true solitude.
- After ten minutes, ask them to finish up and come back to the group. Ask them if they thought that task was difficult. It will come naturally to some more than others.
- Encourage them to try to do this at least three times a week to create a time to pray and listen to God.

LEADER DEVOTIONAL:

Key Verse:

"Do not be anxious about anything, but in every situation, by prayer and petition, with thanksgiving, present your requests to God. And the peace of God, which transcends all understanding, will guard your hearts and your minds in Christ Jesus."

Philippians 4:6-7

There have been times in my life when I have wondered if it even mattered to pray. Does God listen to my words? Does He care about every detail? The answer is a resounding YES! He does listen and He does care, even when we may think our words are empty. God instructs us to pray to Him and to be devoted to this practice of prayer (Colossians 4:2). Often times, prayer is more for us to acknowledge our position with God. He wants us to depend on Him for all things: health, family, job, and daily life! Being devoted to prayer allows us to rejoice, persevere through struggles, and keep our focus on the Lord. Let us be devoted to prayer today, and we can rest assured that God hears us, knows us, and wants the best for us in His kingdom.

In this lesson, you will be challenging the girls in your group to the following beauty tip and action challenge. We encourage you to do these for yourself first, so you can testify to the girls about what kind of impact they had on your heart, mind, soul, and strength.

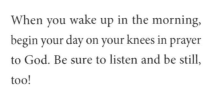

When you wake up in the morning, begin your day on your knees in prayer to God. Be sure to listen and be still, too!

Plan a time every day this week to spend some quiet time with God in the Bible and in prayer.

key takeaways

session seven

cultivating a servant heart

Overcoming the busy disease to love others right where they are.

INTRODUCTION TO TOPIC:

Our sole purpose in this life is to love. First, we are loved by God, and then out His love for us, we love others. We have learned that our worth is in Christ, and because of that, we can make pure choices and we can have confidence and strength through God and who he is making us to be. Once we have these things in place, we can focus fully on our mission to serve others out of love. We serve by using the unique passions and talents that God has gifted to us in the places God has placed us.

STRUGGLES AT THIS AGE:

A big struggle at this age for girls is that they are completely wrapped up in their own world. Grasping the need to serve others will be a difficult one. As we have examined all along, teens are going through a lot. It is hard to go through those things and think of others. But this is also a crucial age for teens to serve. They are malleable and can learn a lot in serving. Teens often have ideas of how to serve, but are limited by the adults in their life. I would encourage you to be cautious of this and also be cautious of dampening young spirits.

ACTIVITY IDEAS:

Hand or feet washing
- ◆ **Materials Needed:**
  - ▪ Tubs or large bowls with warm water
  - ▪ Washcloths (one for each girl)
- ◆ Have the girls take turns washing each others hands and feet
- ◆ Discuss this activity
- ◆ Was it awkward or a little gross to wash someone else's feet? Why? (Be open and honest—feet are normally dirty—it is okay to admit that it was gross.)
- ◆ Was it easier to wash someone else's feet or let someone wash your feet?
- ◆ Serving can be like this. Sometimes, it is awkward, sometimes it causes us to get on our knees or get our hands dirty. Are there times when you would rather just skip helping all together?
- ◆ Read John 13:1-7 together. Washing feet was a job for a servant. Sometimes God may ask us to do jobs we feel should be for someone else. But here, He sets the example for us. When we put others before ourselves, we can show others Christ's love.

Service Project
- ◆ **Materials Needed:**
  - ▪ Spiritual Gifts inventories from Session 2
- ◆ Have the girls consider how they can use their spiritual gifts to serve others, specifically, right where they are. Share with the

group. Now discuss the needs of your community, and how the group as a whole could serve.

* Choose a way to serve together. Have the girls brainstorm ideas of what they would like to do by using their talents, passions, and opportunities.
* Help guide the girls in their brainstorming, but be cautious to guide too much or squash their spirits.
* Create a timeline of details that need to be determined. If you are able, set a date to do the service project.

• See wrap-up activity *Destroy the Destroyer's Influence over You,* in Session 8 if you do not plan to meet again.

LEADER DEVOTIONAL:

Key Verse:

Jesus replied: "'Love the Lord your God with all your heart and with all your soul and with all your mind.' This is the first and greatest commandment. And the second is like it: 'Love your neighbor as yourself.'

Matthew 22:37 – 38

Many things in the Bible are backwards to what the world may say and think. God wants us to do things differently. Being great is not about rising to the top of the corporate world or being the "best" at all things. No, being great in God's eyes means being a servant (Matthew 20:26). Jesus Himself lived this servant lifestyle, and as His followers, we must do the same.

Another example we have of the servant heart is found in our beloved Proverbs 31 woman. Verse 20 of Proverbs 31 says she opens her arms to the poor and extends her hands to the needy. This tells us she is making a conscious effort to help those who are less fortunate than her. It doesn't say that she threw money at them. No, she was involved in their lives. How often do you take the time to look around for those that may be in need, and actually do something about it? Probably not as often as we should. But whenever we have the opportunity, we need to do good for all (Galatians 6:10). Remember too, that "poor and needy" doesn't have to mean money. It can mean any kind of need, whether that be emotional, physical, mental, spiritual.

As we become older, service becomes more natural than it is for teens, and often, our problem is serving too much, rather than not enough. So, if you are feeling worn out from serving others, take heart. God tells us that the harvest is coming, and our job is to not give up from day to day. Let us serve our way to greatness today, by paying attention to people in our lives who we can help.

In this lesson, you will be challenging the girls in your group to the following beauty tip and action challenge. We encourage you to do these for yourself first, so you can testify to the girls about what kind of impact they had on your heart, mind, soul, and strength.

action challenge

What are you passionate about in life? What talents do you feel God has blessed you with to help others? List the ways in which you can use those talents to serve.

beauty tip

If your heart nudges you toward someone in need, act right then—don't wait. You never know what that person may be going through at that time.

key takeaways

reflect AND respond

We encourage you to meet again to discuss all that the girls have learned. While we believe every woman and girl needs the messages in this book, each group will have a different dynamic and each individual a different journey. This additional meeting will allow you the opportunity to ask the girls if they have any more questions and to dig deeper into any of the areas you see fit.

Consider having a bonfire with the activity below, or just a fun wrap-up party. Talk about walls that you are beginning to tear down and ways you can continue to mentor and love on one another.

The service project recommended in Session 7 could be done on the same day as your final session, or you could make them into two additional outings or sessions together.

Destroy the Destroyer's Influence over You!
- ◆ **Materials Needed:**
  - ▪ Sealed envelopes from Session One
  - ▪ Trash Can or fire pit/Campfire
- ◆ Pass out envelopes from the first lesson.
- ◆ Discuss what the girls have learned. Allow time for all to share.

- Discuss how the labels and negative thoughts they wrote down weeks ago are lies Satan wants us to believe. But we now know that our worth is found in Christ.
- Have each girl rip up her envelope and place in trash. Or if you are really into it, burn them in a fire. Celebrate each girl's uniqueness!

Finally, THANK YOU!

Thank you for your heart for these teen girls. Teens, as you know, are highly impressionable. As as our world continues to change, it will likely become increasingly difficult for teen girls to find mentors and real friendships where they can turn when they are feeling alone, broken, rejected or lost.

So on behalf of all of us at P31 Fitness THANK YOU *for* YOUR *servant heart and willingness to give of your time to help us spread this message to teen girls everywhere! We are grateful for you! We hope you feel like you have gotten something out of this study as well, and that you too can remember that you are enough, and that you are worthy because* HE *says you are!*

Please feel free to reach out to us by email at worthit@p31fitness.com. We would love to hear from you on how your journey went.

Thank you again!

Sincerely,

Rachel Curtis (Founder)
And contributors

Made in the USA
Coppell, TX
10 February 2022

73319611R00056